Northern Star Quilt

Sue Bouchard

To Dylan,
May the Stars from Heaven Guide Your Heart and Soul.
Love Mom

Supplies

- 6" x 24" Ruler
- 6" x 12" Ruler
- Small Flying Geese Ruler (Wallhanging/Lap Robe)
- Large Flying Geese Ruler (Queen/King Size)
- Stiletto

- Rotary Cutter and Mat
- Marking Pen or Quilter's Pencil
- Neutral Thread
- ¼" Foot
- Walking Foot

The quilt can be made in four sizes by choosing either the Small or Large Flying Geese Ruler.

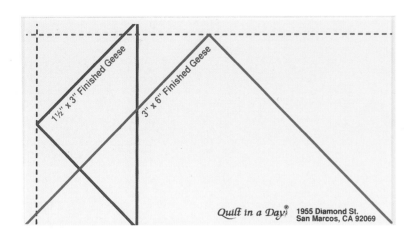

Use the small ruler for Lap Robe and Wallhanging.

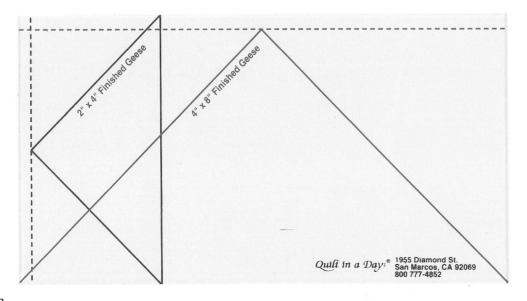

Use the large ruler for the Queen and King size quilt.

Rulers will not slide when cutting if you place four fabric grips on the underside of your ruler.

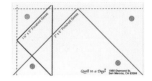

Yardage and Cutting Charts

Wallhanging

Sue Bouchard · Wallhanging – 42" x 42"

Background   ½ yard

Small and Large Stars
Cut (2) 3½" strips into
(16) 3½" squares
Cut (1) 2" strip into
(20) 2" squares
Cut (1) 4½" strip into
(5) 4½" squares

Light   ¾ yard

Large Star
Cut (2) 7½" strips into
(6) 7½" squares

Pieced Border - Stars
Cut (1) 3½" strip into
(4) 3½" squares
Cut (1) 6" strip into
(4) 6" squares

First Medium   1 yard

Small Stars
Cut (1) 6" strip into
(5) 6" squares
Cut (1) 3½" strip into
(5) 3½" squares

Pieced Border
Cut (4) 3½" strips
Cut (2) 4½" squares

Second Medium   ¼ yard

Large Star Centers
Cut (1) 6½" strip into
(4) 6½" squares

Dark   1¼ yards

Large Star Points
Cut (2) 9" strips into
(6) 9" squares

Pieced Border
Cut (9) 2" strips
Cut (1) into (16) 2" squares
Cut (2) 4½" squares

Binding   ½ yard
Cut (5) 3" strips

Batting/Backing   48" x 48"

3

Lap Robe

Lap Robe – 60" x 78"

Background   1¼ yards

Small and Large Stars
> Cut (5) 3½" strips into
>> (48) 3½" squares
>
> Cut (4) 2" strips into
>> (72) 2" squares
>
> Cut (2) 4½" strips into
>> (18) 4½" squares

Light   1½ yards

Large Star
> Cut (5) 7½" strips into
>> (21) 7½" squares

Pieced Border - Stars
> Cut (1) 3½" strip into
>> (4) 3½" squares
>
> Cut (1) 6" strip into
>> (4) 6" squares

First Medium   1¾ yards

Small Stars
> Cut (3) 6" strips into
>> (18) 6" squares
>
> Cut (2) 3½" strips into
>> (18) 3½" squares

Pieced Border
> Cut (7) 3½" strips
> Cut (2) 4½" squares

Second Medium   ¾ yard

Large Star Centers
> Cut (3) 6½" strips into
>> (17) 6½" squares

Dark   2¾ yards

Large Star Points
> Cut (6) 9" strips into
>> (21) 9" squares

Pieced Border
> Cut (15) 2" strips
>> Cut (1) into (16) 2" squares
> Cut (2) 4½" squares

Binding   ¾ yard
> Cut (7) 3" strips

Batting/Backing   68" x 86"

Queen/King Quilt

Background   1¾ yards

Small and Large Stars
  Cut (6) 4½" strips into
      (48) 4½" squares
  Cut (5) 2½" strips into
      (72) 2½" squares
  Cut (3) 5½" strips into
      (18) 5½" squares

Light   2¼ yards

Large Star
  Cut (6) 9½" strips into
      (21) 9½" squares
Pieced Border – Stars
  Cut (1) 4½" strip into
      (4) 4½" squares
  Cut (1) 7" strip into
      (4) 7" squares

First Medium   2¾ yards

Small Stars
  Cut (4) 7" strips into
      (18) 7" squares
  Cut (3) 4½" strips into
      (18) 4½" squares
Pieced Border
  Cut (9) 4½" strips
  Cut (2) 5½" squares

Second Medium   1½ yards

Large Star Centers
  Cut (5) 8½" strips into
      (17) 8½" squares

Queen – 86" x 110"   *King – 92" x 116"*

Dark   5 yards (Queen) or 6 yards (King)

Large Star Points
  Cut (7) 11" strips into
      (21) 11" squares
Pieced Border
  Cut (19) 2½" strips
      Cut (1) into (16) 2½" squares
  Cut (2) 5½" squares
Second Border – Queen Size
  Cut (11) 3½" strips
Second Border – King Size
  Cut (11) 6½" strips

Binding   1 yard
  Cut (10) 3" strips for Queen
  Cut (11) 3" strips for King

Batting/Backing   94" x 118" for Queen
                    100" x 124" for King

General Instructions for Flying Geese Patches

1. Place the smaller square right sides together and centered on the larger square. Press.

2. With the 6" x 24" ruler, draw a diagonal line across the squares. Pin.

3. Sew exactly ¼" from both sides of drawn line. Press to set seam.

4. Cut on drawn line.

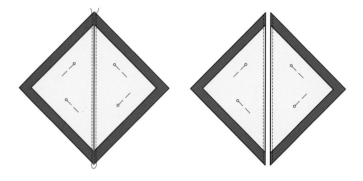

5. Place on pressing mat with larger triangle on top. Set seams, open, and press seams to larger triangle.

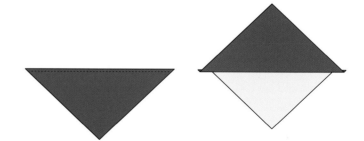

6. Place squares right sides together so that opposite fabrics touch.

7. Match up the outside edges. Notice that there is a gap between the seams. The seams do not lock.

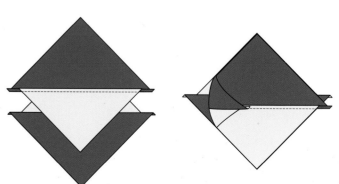

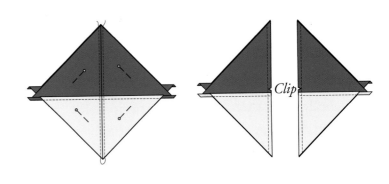

8. Draw a diagonal line across the seams. Pin.

9. Sew ¼" from both sides of drawn line. Press to set seam.

10. Cut on the drawn line. Clip the seam allowance to the vertical seam midway between the horizontal seams.

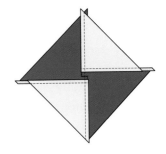

11. Press each half open, pushing the clipped seam allowance to the fabric of the larger square.

12. Place the Geese on a small cutting mat so you can rotate the mat as you cut. Select the correct ruler.

13. Line up the ruler's lines on the 45° sewn lines. Line up the dotted line with the peak of the triangle for the ¼" seam allowance.

14. Cut the block in half to separate the two patches.

3" x 6" and 4" x 8" rulers horizontal

3" x 6" and 4" x 8" Geese:
Trim off excess fabric on all four sides, turning the mat as you cut. Hold the ruler securely on your fabric so it will not shift while you are cutting.

1½" x 3" and 2" x 4" Geese:
Trim off excess fabric.

Turn the patch around. **Do not turn the ruler.** Trim off excess fabric.

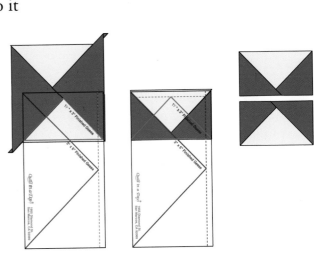

1½" x 3" and 2" x 4" rulers vertical

Making Small Stars *Color of illustrations follow the Queen/King quilt.*

1. Place smaller squares right sides together to larger squares.

2. Following the General instructions for the Flying Geese patch, make Flying Geese patches.

		Wallhanging	Lap Robe	Queen/King
	Background	(5) 4½" squares	(18) 4½" squares	(18) 5½" squares
	First Medium	(5) 6" squares	(18) 6" squares	(18) 7" squares
	Square to	2" x 3½"	2" x 3½"	2½" x 4½"
	Number of Geese	20	72	72

3. Place patches in stacks equal to the number of stars.

		Wallhanging	Lap Robe	Queen/King
	Number of Stars	5	18	18
	Background Corners	(20) 2" squares	(72) 2" squares	(72) 2½" squares
	First Medium Center	(5) 3½" squares	(18) 3½" squares	(18) 4½" squares
	Flying Geese	(20) 2" x 3½"	(72) 2" x 3½"	(72) 2½" x 4½"

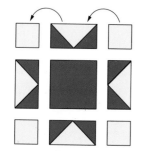 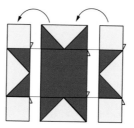 

4. Assembly line sew pieces right sides together into rows. Clip apart between blocks.

5. Press seams away from Flying Geese patches. Sew the rows right sides together.

6. Press seams away from center.

7. **Wallhanging:** Set one Star aside for Cornerstones.

8. **Lap Robe and Queen:** Set six Stars aside for Cornerstones.

9. **Star Sizes:** Wallhanging 6½", Lap Robe 6½", Queen/King 8½"

Making Large Star Points

1. Place smaller squares right sides together to larger squares.

2. Following the General Instructions for the Flying Geese patch, make Flying Geese patches.

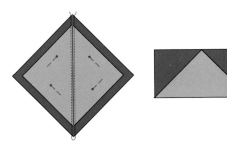

		Wallhanging	Lap Robe	Queen/King
⬜	Light	(6) 7½" squares	(21) 7½" squares	(21) 9½" squares
⬛	Dark	(6) 9" squares	(21) 9" squares	(21) 11" squares
	Square to	3½" x 6½"	3½" x 6½"	4½" x 8½"
◢◣	Number of Geese	24	84	84

3. Lay out patches with Small Stars. Place patches in stacks equal to the number of stars.

		Wallhanging	Lap Robe	Queen/King
✴	Small Stars	4	12	12
⬜	Background Corners	(16) 3½" squares	(48) 3½" squares	(48) 4½" squares
◢◣	Flying Geese	(16) 3½" x 6½"	(48) 3½" x 6½"	(48) 4½" x 8½"

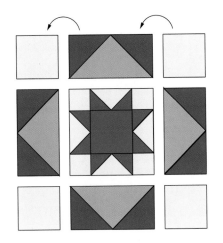

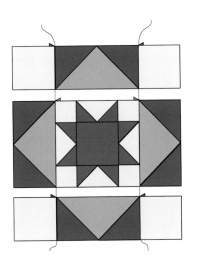

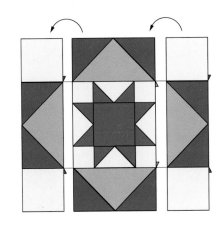

4. Assembly-line sew pieces right sides together. **Clip apart between blocks.**

5. Press seams away from Flying Geese patches.

6. Sew rows together.

7. Press seams away from center.

Making the Large Star Centers

1. Lay out patches for the Large Star Centers.

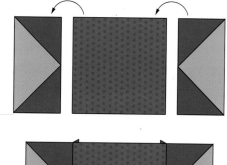

2. Assembly-line sew. Press seams toward center square.

		Wallhanging	Lap Robe	Queen/King
	Second Medium	(4) 6½" squares	(17) 6½" squares	(17) 8½" squares
	Flying Geese	(8) 3½" x 6½"	(34) 3½" x 6½"	(34) 4½" x 8½"

Completing the Quilt Top

1. Lay out Large Star Points and Centers, and Small Stars for Cornerstones.

2. Sew into Rows, and then sew Rows together.

Wallhanging

Lap Robe and Queen/King

Making Four Corner Blocks

1. Count out 2 First Medium smaller squares and 2 Light larger squares, and center right sides together.

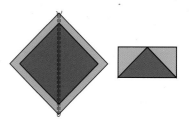

2. Count out 2 Dark smaller squares and 2 Light larger squares, and center right sides together.

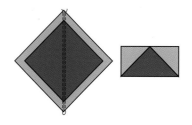

3. Following the General Instructions for the Flying Geese patch, make 8 Flying Geese patches in each color.

		Wallhanging	Lap Robe	Queen/King
	First Medium	(2) 4½" squares	(2) 4½" squares	(2) 5½" squares
	Dark	(2) 4½" squares	(2) 4½" squares	(2) 5½" squares
	Light	(4) 6" squares	(4) 6" squares	(4) 7" squares
	Flying Geese	(8) 2" x 3½"	(8) 2" x 3½"	(8) 2½" x 4½"
	Flying Geese	(8) 2" x 3½"	(8) 2" x 3½"	(8) 2½" x 4½"

4. Lay out patches needed to complete the Border Corners. Place 4 patches in each stack.

		Wallhanging	Lap Robe	Queen/King
	Light	(4) 3½" squares	(4) 3½" squares	(4) 4½" squares
	Dark	(16) 2" squares	(16) 2" squares	(16) 2½" squares
	Flying Geese	(8) 2" x 3½"	(8) 2" x 3½"	(8) 2½" x 4½"
	Flying Geese	(8) 2" x 3½"	(8) 2" x 3½"	(8) 2½" x 4½"

5. Assembly-line sew pieces.

6. Sew rows right sides together. Clip apart between blocks. Press seams away from Flying Geese.

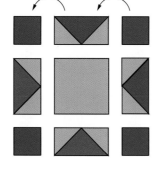
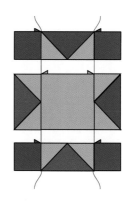
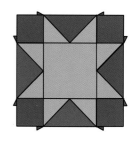

Making Borders

Wallhanging

1. No piecing is required to make strips longer.

Lap Robe

1. Cut one 3½" Medium strip in half. Piece to two 3½" strips for top and bottom. Piece remaining four strips in pairs for both sides.

2. Cut two 2" Dark strips in half. Piece to four 2" strips for top and bottom. Piece remaining eight strips in pairs for both sides.

Queen/King

1. Piece eight 4½" Medium strips into four long strips. Cut remaining strip in half. Piece to two long strips.

2. Piece sixteen 2½" Dark strips into eight long strips. Cut remaining two strips in half. Piece to four long strips.

Sewing Strips Together

1. Sew four strip sets together for Border Sides, Top, and Bottom. Press seams toward Medium.

2. Measure the four sides of your Quilt top and cut Border strips to same size. Pin and sew Side Borders to Quilt top. Press seams toward Border.

3. Sew Four Corner Blocks to Top and Bottom Borders. Press seams toward Border. Sew to Quilt top. Press seams toward Border.

Finishing the Quilt

Wallhanging

1. Backing is ready for layering.

Larger Quilts

1. Cut the backing yardage in two equal pieces.

2. Sew the backing pieces together to make a backing larger than the quilt top.

3. Spread out the backing on a large table or floor area with the right side down. Clamp the fabric to the edge of the table with quilt clips or tape the backing to the floor. Do not stretch the backing.

4. Layer the batting on top of the backing, and pat flat.

5. With the quilt top right side up, center on the backing. Smooth until all layers are flat. Clamp or tape outside edges.

6. Safety pin the layers together every three to five inches. Pin next to your machine quilting lines.

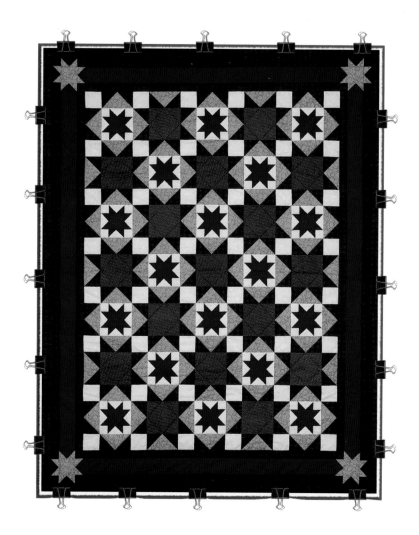

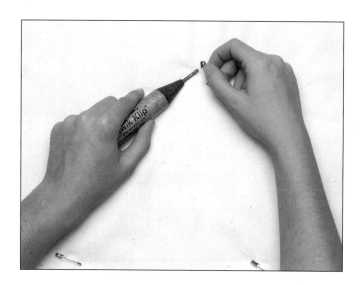

"Stitch in the Ditch" to Anchor the Blocks and Borders

The ideal machine quilting area is a sewing machine bed level with the table, and a large area to the left of the machine to support the quilt. Machine quilt on a day when you are relaxed to help avoid muscle strain down your neck, shoulders, and back. Sit in a raised stenographer's chair so your arms can rest on the table.

1. Attach your walking foot, and lengthen the stitch to 8 to 10 stitches per inch or 3.5 on computerized machines.

2. Roll on the diagonal to the center. Clip the rolls in place.

3. Spread the seams open, and "stitch in the ditch."

4. Unroll the quilt to the next diagonal seam. Clip the roll in place, and "stitch in the ditch."

5. Continue to unroll and roll the quilt until all the seams are stitched, anchoring the blocks.

6. Stitch in the ditch on the border seams.

7. Drop your feed dogs, attach your darning foot and thread your machine with matching thread or invisible thread. If you use invisible thread, loosen your top tension. Match the bobbin thread to the backing.

8. Sew around each of the small stars.

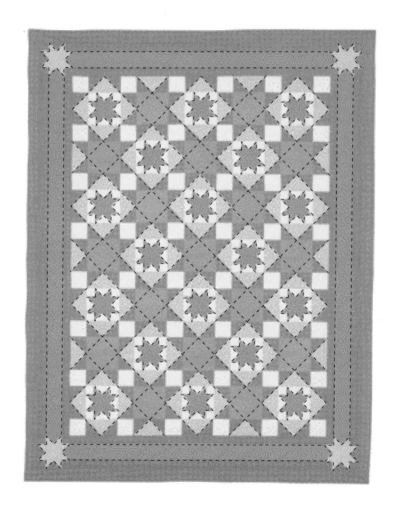

Adding the Binding

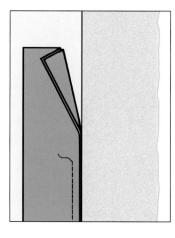

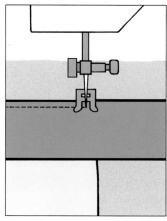

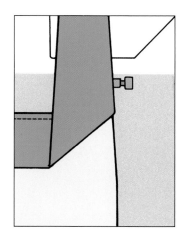

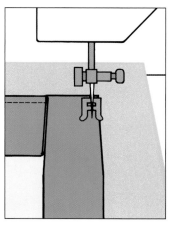

Use a walking foot attachment and regular thread on top and in the bobbin to match the binding.

1. Square off the selvage edges, and sew 3" strips together lengthwise.

2. Fold and press in half with wrong sides together.

3. Line up the raw edges of the folded binding with the raw edges of the quilt in the middle of one side. Begin stitching 4" from the end of the binding.

4. At the corner, stop the stitching ¼" from the edge with the needle in the fabric. Raise the presser foot and turn the quilt to the next side. Put the foot back down.

5. Stitch backwards ¼" to the edge of the binding, raise the foot, and pull the quilt forward slightly.

6. Fold the binding strip straight up on the diagonal. Fingerpress the diagonal fold.

7. Fold the binding strip straight down with the diagonal fold underneath. Line up the top of the fold with the raw edge of the binding underneath.

8. Begin sewing from the edge.

9. Continue stitching and mitering the corners around the outside of the quilt.

10. Stop stitching 4" from where the ends will overlap.

11. Line up the two ends of binding. Trim the excess with a ½" overlap.

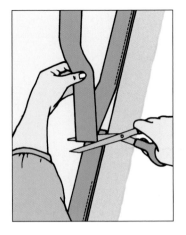

12. Open out the folded ends and pin right sides together. Sew a ¼" seam.

13. Continue to stitch the binding in place.

14. Trim the batting and backing up to the raw edges of the binding.

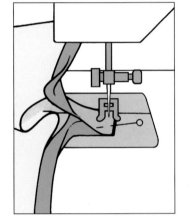

15. Fold the binding to the back side of the quilt. Pin in place so that the folded edge on the binding covers the stitching line. Tuck in the excess fabric at each miter on the diagonal.

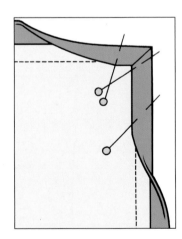

16. From the right side, "stitch in the ditch" using invisible thread on the front side, and a bobbin thread to match the binding on the back side. Catch the folded edge of the binding on the back side with the stitching.

17. Optional: Hand stitch on the back side.

18. Sew on identification label.

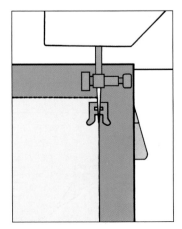